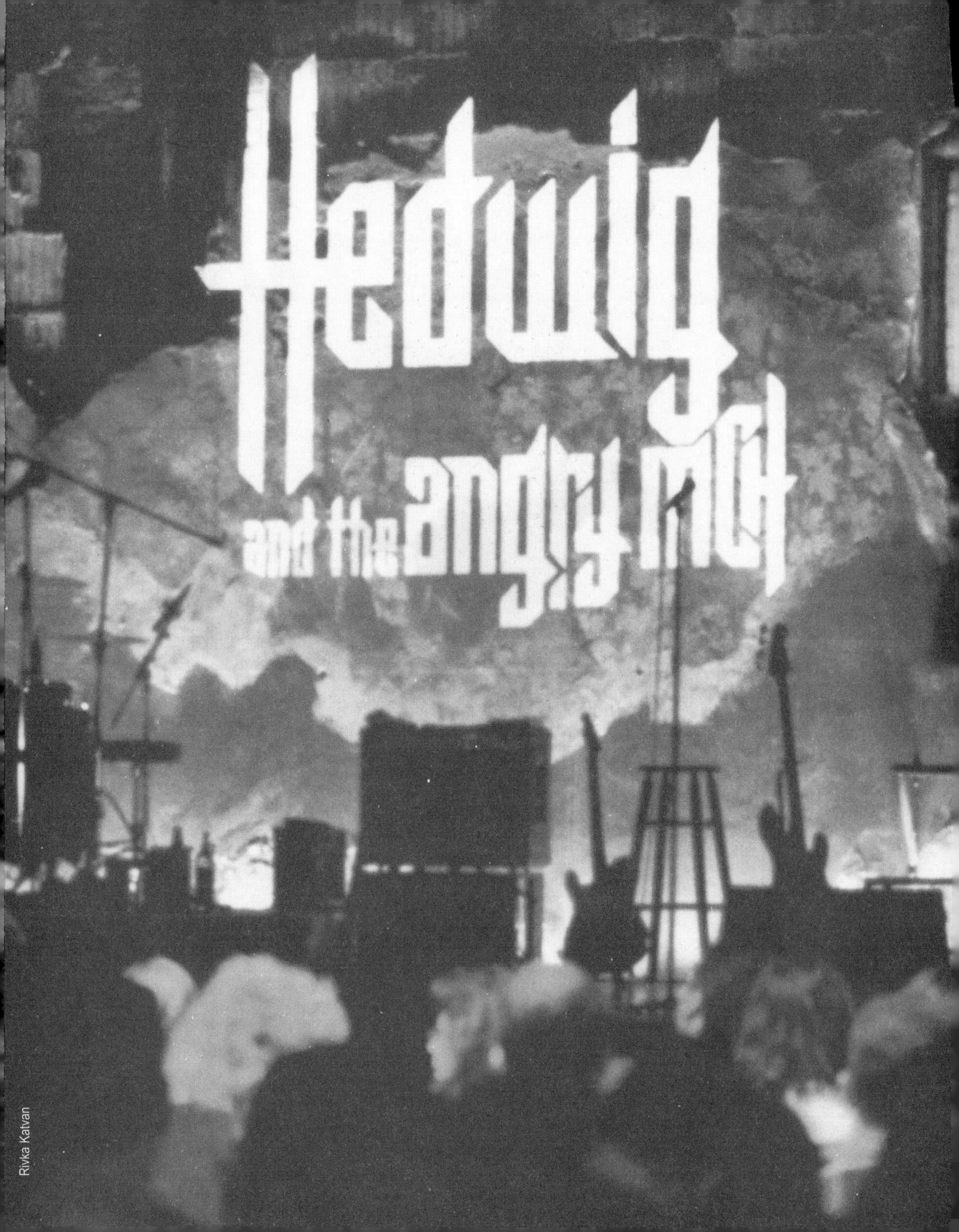

Rivka Katvan

Hedwig
AND THE ANGRY INCH

Text John Cameron Mitchell   Music & Lyrics Stephen Trask

Photographs Rivka Katvan   Carol Rosegg

THE OVERLOOK PRESS
WOODSTOCK & NEW YORK

First published in the United States in 2000 by
The Overlook Press, Peter Mayer Publishers, Inc.
Lewis Hollow Road
Woodstock, New York 12498
www.overlookpress.com

Library of Congress Cataloging-in-Publication Data

Trask, Stephen.
[Hedwig and the Angry Inch. Libretto]
Hedwig and the Angry Inch : the complete play and lyrics to the cult smash /
John Cameron Mitchell; [music &] lyrics by Stephen Trask; photographs by Rivka Katvan
and Carol Rosegg

BOOK DESIGN AND FORMATTING BY BERNARD SCHLEIFER
LOGO DESIGN BY GREY ENTERTAINMENT/DANIELLE PONCHERI
Manufactured in the United States of America
FIRST EDITION
1 3 5 7 9 8 6 4 2
ISBN 1-58567-034-0

Hedwig and The Angry Inch was originally presented at the Westbeth Theatre Center on February 27, 1997 by David Binder. It was presented off-Broadway at the Jane Street Theatre on February 14, 1998 by Peter Askin, Susann Brinkley, James B. Freydberg.

The cast was as follows:

Hedwig/Tommy Gnosis .	John Cameron Mitchell
Yitzhak	Miriam Shor
The Angry Inch	Cheater, comprised of Stephen Trask, Chris Weilding, Dave McKinley, Scott Bilbrey

Directed by Peter Askin
Set by James Youmans
Lighting by Kevin Adams

AUTHORS' NOTE

This script is, at best, a record of a single evening of a single production of *Hedwig and the Angry Inch*. We deliberately developed it over a number of years in non-theatrical venues— rock clubs, drag bars, birthday parties, friends' patios—in order to keep it free-flowing, improvisational, alive. We encourage other productions to keep this sense of freedom by ad-libbing when appropriate within the confines of the world of the piece. This script reflects that we were performing at the Hotel Riverview where survivors of the Titanic actually stayed. Tommy Gnosis was therefore "performing" nearby at Giants Stadium. We feel that every production should be site-specific so that the character of Hedwig is actually performing in and commenting on the space the production is occupying. Feel free to change the text to accommodate the environment. Just be witty, damn it!

JOHN CAMERON MITCHELL
STEPHEN TRASK

(A riverside fleabag hotel ballroom with a stage at one end. Upstage is an emergency exit door. Projected on the back wall of the stage is a rock and roll band logo: Hedwig and The Angry Inch. *Already on stage is* The Angry Inch, *a tacky rock band dressed flashily in 80's high style, lots of shoulderpads and stone-washed denim.* YITZHAK, *a sullen male roadie, trudges to the center stage mike.)*

YITZHAK

(in an Eastern European accent)

Ladies and gentlemen, whether you like it or not . . . Hedwig.

*(*Oh, Beautiful *begins on majestic solo guitar and* HEDWIG *enters down the center aisle. She is wrapped in a full length acid-washed denim cape inspired by the American flag. Black light floods the stage as she takes it. She whips open the cape to reveal a lining painted to look like a wall. Shining fluorescently are the spray-painted words "Yankee go home with me.")*

Rivka Katvan

HEDWIG

Don't you know me? I'm the new Berlin Wall. Try and tear me down!

TEAR ME DOWN

*(illustrated by a projected montage of
images of the Berlin Wall)*

*I was born on the other side
of a town ripped in two
I made it over the great divide
Now I'm coming for you*

*Enemies and adversaries
they try and tear me down
You want me, baby, I dare you
Try and tear me down*

*I rose from off of the doctor's slab
like Lazarus from the pit
Now everyone wants to take a stab
and decorate me
with blood graffiti and spit*

*Enemies and adversaries
they try and tear me down
You want me, baby, I dare you
Try and tear me down*

YITZHAK

(who has been singing backup, shouts out:)

On August 13, 1961,

a wall was erected

down the middle of the city of Berlin.

The world was divided by a cold war

and the Berlin wall

was the most hated symbol of that divide

Reviled. Graffitied. Spit upon.

We thought the wall would stand forever,

and now that it's gone,

we don't know who we are anymore.

Ladies and Gentleman,

Hedwig is like that wall,

standing before you in the divide

between East and West,

Slavery and Freedom,

Man and Woman,

Top and Bottom.

And you can try and tear her down,

but before you do,

remember one thing.

HEDWIG

Listen

There ain't much of a difference

between a bridge and a wall

Without me right in the middle, babe
you would be nothing at all

Enemies and adversaries
they try and tear me down
You want me, baby, I dare you
try and tear me down.

*(*YITZHAK *upstages* HEDWIG *with a fabulous high note.* HEDWIG *pulls the cable out of his mike and regains supremacy.)*

HEDWIG

. . . down!

(Big arena rock finish!)

HEDWIG

Thank you! Thank you, you're so sweet. I do love a warm hand on my entrance. My name is Hedwig. Please welcome The Angry Inch! And my man Friday through Thursday, Yitzhak! *(stepping on* YITZHAK's *applause)* There's really no need. There's none. I'm thrilled you could join me for this special opening night performance here at the beautiful Hotel Riverview. *(an ad slogan:* "Hotel Riverview—you can really view the river!"*)* This grand ballroom has a celebrated history as a place of sanctuary . . . of succor, if you will . . . having once sheltered the surviving crew of the Titanic. Perhaps they can hear me now. *(addressing them)* You brave unfortunate souls—blasted by man's hubris and washed up on cruel shores—I, who am simply blasted and washed up, salute you! Welcome to the fabulous first night of my unlimited New York run. And when it comes to huge openings, a lot of people think of me. Many more of you, though, have only recently become aware of me.

(She refers to a projected New York Post *cover dominated by a police mugshot of a bandaged young man with a silver cross painted on his forehead. The man bears a remarkable likeness to* HEDWIG. *The headline reads:* "TOMMY TO TOTS: I'M SORRY!"*)*

It took a tragedy to make you finally pay attention. But now you're interested. Intrigued even.

(Projection zooms to a tiny box at the bottom of the page featuring a smiling mugshot of a bandaged HEDWIG *with the caption,* "Who is Mystery Woman?"*)*

(in a broad American accent) Who is this Hedwig and why have we never heard about her before, Bob? *(back to her normal accent)* Well, that's a question I've been asking myself for years minus the Bob. How did some slip of a girlyboy from communist East Berlin become the internationally ignored song stylist barely standing before you? That's what I want to talk about tonight. I'm not here to talk about calamity or scandal. I'm not here to talk about my relationship with a certain well-known rock icon, Tommy Gnosis . . . . *(projection zooms to man's mugshot)* Even though, at this very moment, he's probably talking about me. By some freak coincidence, he's previewing his "Tour of Atonement" tonight at Giants Stadium, right across the river.

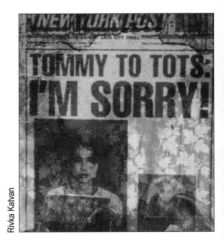

Rivka Katvan

(She pushes open the upstage emergency exit door. Blinding light pours in. We hear arena-sized cheers . . .)

TOMMY *(off)*

. . . Hello New York! Listen . . . listen . . . there's someone I want to thank for the way they've handled this tragedy . . . With incredible loyalty in the face of a lot of lies. And that someone is . . .

(HEDWIG draws herself up.)

TOMMY *(off)*

. . . you! My fans!

(Her face falls. The crowd cheers. A cheesy intro to Tear Me Down *begins.)*

TOMMY *(off)*

. . . and together, no one's gonna tear us down!

(sings:)
Enemies and adversaries
they try and tear me down—

(HEDWIG slams the door.)

HEDWIG

I wrote every song on that album! And by the way, the tabloids got it right. He *was* driving, he *was* on blow, he *was* getting blown by yours truly, and he *did* hit the schoolbus full of deaf children. One survived,—now blind. I taught him everything he knows—and has apparently forgotten—about rock and roll and he barely mentions my name on that giant sucking sound Larry King calls a show, which I'm sure you all saw because if you hadn't, I'd be singing to the desk clerk and, if I was lucky, my agent, Phyllis Stein—did you make it this time, Phyllis? *(She is overcome. She recovers.)*

I'm sorry. I'm wide open tonight.

(projected zoom to HEDWIG'S *mugshot)*

You see, the road is my home. My home, the road. And when I think of all the people I have come upon in my travels, I have to think about the people who have come upon me.

(projected childlike drawings on a Berlin-like wall illuminate the following)

The geography of human contact, the triangulation of a pair of eyes on my face, the latitude and longitude of a hand on my body. These are the only clues I have to my place in the world. To who I am. Who is Mystery Woman!? *(laughs)* I laugh, because I will cry if I don't.

I recently found my first diary, age 2 through 6, fully illustrated *(referring to the projected drawings)* . . . And I realized that so many people have touched me on my way to this stage tonight. How can I say who touched me the most? My father? . . .

(projection of a crude drawing of a dad and little boy holding hands)

The American G.I.? . . . Who left when I was barely old enough to speak my first words: "Daddy, when I grow up, I'll kill you"? Could it have been my East German mother?

(projection of a mom and little boy not holding hands)

No, when she touched me it was usually by accident. Reaching for the beans at the table or something. One day, we were watching *Jesus Christ Superstar* on American Forces Television.

(a crude drawing of the face of Jesus on a T.V. screen)

I turned to Mother:

(HEDWIG *as child:)* "Jesus said the darndest things."

She slapped me.

(MOM*:)* "Don't you ever mention that name to me again."

(HEDWIG *as child:)* "But He died for our sins."

(MOM:) "So did Hitler."

(HEDWIG *as child:)* "What?"

(MOM:) "Absolute power corrupts."

(HEDWIG *as child:)* "Absolutely!"

(MOM:) "Better to be powerless, my son."

She got her wish when the Wall went up.

(Jesus gets glasses but loses hair. Suddenly He's Vladimir Lenin on the T.V.)

We happened to be living on the East side and mother was given a job teaching sculpture to limbless children. Socialism, God rest its soul!

(She repairs to a booth with a table.)

Most of my time was spent listening to American Forces Radio. Our apartment was so small that mother made me play it in the oven. Late at night, I would rest my head on the top rack . . . *(rests her head on the table)* And listen to the American masters . . . Toni Tenille! . . . Debby Boone! . . . Anne Murray! . . . who was actually a Canadian working in the American idiom. Then there were the crypto-homo rockers: Lou Reed! . . . Iggy Pop! . . . David Bowie! . . . who was actually an idiom working in America and Canada. These artists left as deep an impression on me as that oven rack did on my face. To be a young American in muskrat love soft as an easy chair, not even the chair, I am I said! Have I never been mellow? Have I never tried? And the colored girls sing . . . .

YITZHAK

Doo do doo . . .

HEDWIG

I sang along.

YITZHAK & HEDWIG

. . . doo do doo . . . .

HEDWIG

But never with the melody. How could I do it better than Toni or Debby?

YITZHAK

. . . doo do doo . . . .

HEDWIG

Once I couldn't resist: *(singing from* You Light Up My Life*)* "It can't be wrong, if it feels so—!" Mother threw a tomato at my head.

YITZHAK

. . . doo do doo . . . .

HEDWIG

But I was really quite content to sing gentle backup harmonies in my oven.

YITZHAK

. . . doo do doo . . . .

HEDWIG

While mother sculpted in the shower.

YITZHAK

Doo do doo.

(YITZHAK *stops singing.*)

HEDWIG

When the hour grew late and it was time for bed, she would shout from the bathroom, "Well, that's me!" And I would reply from the kitchen, "Well, I guess that's me too." We would wash our feet and brush our teeth and lay down on the narrow pallet that we had shared since Daddy left . . . .

(a drawing of two figures lying uncomfortably back to back)

. . . like two pieces of a puzzle that don't quite fit but are jammed together and left on a table by . . . *(railing at the heavens)* . . . some dangerous shut-in with too much time on his hands!

(gentle guitar intro begins)

I'm sorry, I'm completely dilated right now. I'd like to share with you a bedtime story that mother once whispered to me in the dark and later retracted. Whatever allowed her to reveal such a story to such a little boy, I'll never know. But I remember it like it happened yesterday.

THE ORIGIN OF LOVE

(Crude drawings illustrate the story.)

When the earth was still flat,
And clouds made of fire,
And mountains stretched up to the sky,
Sometimes higher,
Folks roamed the earth
Like big rolling kegs.
They had two sets of arms.
They had two sets of legs.
They had two faces peering
Out of one giant head
So they could watch all around them
As they talked; while they read.
And they never knew nothing of love.
It was before the origin of love.

The origin of love

And there were three sexes then,
One that looked like two men
Glued up back to back,
Called the children of the sun.
And similar in shape and girth
Were the children of the earth.
They looked like two girls
Rolled up in one.

And the children of the moon
Looked like a fork shoved on a spoon.
They were part sun, part earth,
Part daughter, part son.

The origin of love.

Now the gods grew quite scared
Of our strength and defiance
And Thor said,
"I'm gonna kill them all
With my hammer,
Like I killed the giants."
And Zeus said, "No,
You better let me
Use my lightning, like scissors,
Like I cut the legs off the whales
And dinosaurs into lizards."
Then he grabbed up some bolts
And he let out a laugh,
Said, "I'll split them right down the middle.
Gonna cut them right up in half."
And then storm clouds gathered above
Into great balls of fire

And then fire shot down
From the sky in bolts
Like shining blades

Of a knife.
And it ripped
Right through the flesh
Of the children of the sun
And the moon
And the earth.
And some Indian god
Sewed the wound up into a hole,
Pulled it round to our belly
To remind us of the price we pay.
And Osiris and the gods of the Nile
Gathered up a big storm
To blow a hurricane,
To scatter us away,
In a flood of wind and rain,
And a sea of tidal waves,
To wash us all away,
And if we don't behave
They'll cut us down again
And we'll be hopping around on one foot
And looking through one eye.

Last time I saw you
We had just split in two.
You were looking at me.
I was looking at you.
You had a way so familiar,
But I could not recognize,

Cause you had blood on your face;
I had blood in my eyes.
But I could swear by your expression
That the pain down in your soul
Was the same as the one down in mine.
That's the pain,
Cuts a straight line
Down through the heart;
We called it love.
So we wrapped our arms around each other,
Trying to shove ourselves back together.
We were making love,
Making love.
It was a cold dark evening,
Such a long time ago,
When by the mighty hand of Jove,
It was a sad story
How we became
Lonely two-legged creatures,
It's the story of
The origin of love.
That's the origin of love.

After mother finished, she began to snore. But I had to go some-
where I could think. I crept into the kitchen and put my head in the
oven.

It is clear that I must find my other half. But is it a he or a she? Is it

Daddy? He went away. Or Mother? I was suddenly afraid to go back to bed. What does this person look like? Identical to me? Or somehow complementary? Does my other half have what I don't? Did he get the looks, the luck, the love? Were we really separated forcibly or did he just run off with the good stuff? Or did I? Will this person embarrass me? And what about sex? Is that how we put ourselves back together again? Is that what Daddy was trying to do? Or can two people actually become one again? And if we're driving on the Autobahn when it happens, can we still use the diamond lane?

Practical questions of wholeness. Completion. Think of it. I thought of it. I thought of the power. (YITZHAK *holds up a hand mirror.*) The gods were terrified! (HEDWIG *looks in the mirror and recoils.*)

HEDWIG

Magnifying side. Very funny, Yitzhak. Very passive-aggressive. *(points into the house)* Look, Yitzhak, immigration!

(YITZHAK *is deflated.*) If you behave, I might let you shave my back. That will be all. (YITZHAK *seethes off to the side.* HEDWIG *admires herself in the mirror.*)

How's my hair? Is there trouble in the west wing? *(refers to large curls)* These are actually my lungs. My Aquanet lungs. They kick in on the high notes. Now, I want to you to be serious. Just the other day I was telling Yitzhak how nervous I was about tonight . . .

(YITZHAK *has removed a flowing wig from a shelf and is lovingly combing it.*)

(HEDWIG *smooths her denim dress.*)

. . . Would I still be able to fit into that old Sergio Valente? There was no time to diet, so I had my heart removed. Suddenly, I was a perfect size six!

(*She hears* YITZHAK *singing softly and catches him swishing about with the hairpiece on his head.*)

WAS MACHST DU DA VERDAMMT NOCH MAL?

(*A redfaced* YITZHAK *whips the wig back onto the prop shelf.*)

HEDWIG

I'm sorry you had to see that, ladies and gentlemen. When I met him he said he wanted to be a model. A foot model, maybe. Enough about him, let's get back to the—

YITZHAK

(*surreptitiously into a mike*)
Bitch.

HEDWIG

Yes? Did someone call my name? I thought I heard my—

YITZHAK

Bitch.

(HEDWIG *looks back at* YITZHAK. YITZHAK, *as if searching for the source of the voice, opens the emergency door. The* Tommy Gnosis *concert pours in again.*)

TOMMY (*off*)

—I realized there was only one person who had ever really been there for me in my life. And that person was me. The accident was a cry for help. I was yelling "Help!" to me—

(HEDWIG *slams the door.*)

HEDWIG

Well, what about me? Without me he never would've swerved into that oncoming short bus and got all that attention! Let me just take a second here, against the advice of my lawyers, Jacoby, Meyers and Lee Bailey. I had just wrapped up a late-night engagement in the meat-packing district. We're talking about the tony, newly reno-vated, meat-packing district. You've heard of SoHo? NoHo? This is MePa. I was standing there on 14th Street, the very boulevard of MePa, when a limo pulled up. I stepped into it, naturally mistaking it for my own. In the limo sat Tommy Gnosis. We were both aston-ished. It had been years. So we dropped the driver off and drove up and down the island, doing drugs and catching up. We talked about the disappointing sales of his second album—the one he wrote without me. He spoke of his loneliness. I reminded him of happier days. I just couldn't keep my mouth shut and, well, you know the rest. So you can imagine, when the story broke, Tommy's people offered me a small fortune to keep all this to myself. As if I'd accept their filthy lucre. As if selling the story of someone else's pain was my only means of support. As if I hadn't already launched my new fragrance: "Atrocity." By Hedwig.

(*projection of* Atrocity *logo*)

It's a fragrance for a man or a woman. Or a freak. I digress. One day in the late mid eighties . . . I was in my early late twenties. I had just been dismissed from university after delivering a brilliant lecture on the aggressive influence of German philosophy on rock and roll entitled: "You, Kant, Always Get What You Want". At 26, my academic career was over, I had never kissed a boy and I was still sleeping with mom. The search for my other half on this side of the Wall had proved futile. Might he be found on the other?

(projection of drawn figures separated by wall)

But how to get over? People died trying. Such were the thoughts flooding my tiny head on the day that I was sunning myself in an old bomb crater I had discovered near the Wall. I am naked, face down, on a piece of broken church, inhaling a fragrant westerly breeze. The new McDonalds has just opened on the other side. My God, I deserve a break today. All I ever get is the unhappy meal. The sun is hot, but I feel a sudden chill. I look over my shoulder. A head-shaped shadow is resting on the pillow of my ass.

Rivka Katvan

> (LUTHER:) "Girl, I sure don't mean to annoy you. My name is Corporal Luther Robinson."

I turn my body to face him.

> (HEDWIG:) "My name is Hansel."

Luther is silent for a moment as he stares at my little bishop in a turtleneck.

> (LUTHER:) "Hansel. Well. You must like candy."

(HEDWIG:) "I like Gummi Baerchen."

Out of his pocket comes a strange packet that says "Gummy Bears" on it. Gummy Bears? *(projection of bear)* I select a single clear bear. It is the biggest one I've ever seen. The taste is completely different from a Gummi Bear yet it is somehow familiar. It is much sweeter than a Gummi Bear and softer, too. Its little gummy body stretches on the rack of my molars. Wow, I feel so optimistic. What is that flavor? He pours me a handful, his eyes heavy with an unfamiliar desire. Could it be a desire to please? Me? I suddenly recognize the flavor in my mouth. It's the taste of power. Not bad.

(LUTHER:) "Damn, Hansel, I can't believe you're not a girl, you're so fine. Why don't you take the whole bag?"

He searches my face for news of his fate. His expression is echoed in scores of tiny faces pressing against clear plastic. Panting faces of every imaginable color, creed and non-Aryan origin fogging up the bag like the windows of a Polish bathhouse. It's only a shower. Absolute power. *(slaps herself)* I push Luther away and stumble naked through the ruins, back towards blander, less complicated confections, leaving in my wake a trail of rainbow carnage.

Next day, Hansel follows the trail back.

. . . and lying on my slab are three Milky Ways, a roll of Necco Wafers, some Pop Rocks, and a Giant-Size Sugar Daddy named Luther.

(A projection of LUTHER's *and* HEDWIG's *bodies commingling in the shape of a swastika is accompanied by a few bars of* Deutschland Über Alles *which segue into . . .)*

SUGAR DADDY

I've got a sweet tooth
for licorice drops and jelly roll,
Hey sugar daddy,
Hansel needs some sugar in his bowl.
I'll lay out fine china on the linen
and polish up the chrome
and if you got some sugar for me,
Sugar Daddy, bring it home.

Black strap molasses,
you're my orange blossom honey bear.
Bring me Versace blue jeans
and black designer underwear.
Let's dress up like the disco–dancing jet set
in Milan and Rome.
And if you got some sugar for me,
Sugar Daddy, bring it home.

Oh the thrill of control,
like the rush of rock and roll,
is the sweetest taste I've known.
So come on, Sugar Daddy, bring it home.

When honey bees go shopping
it's something to be seen.
They swarm to wild flowers
and get nectar for the queen.
And every gift you bring me
gets me dripping like a honeycomb
and if you got some sugar for me,
Sugar Daddy, bring it home.

Oh the thrill of control,
like a Blitzkrieg on the roll,
is the sweetest taste I've known.
So if you got some sugar
bring it home.
Oh come on, Sugar Daddy bring it home!

Whiskey and French cigarettes,
a motorbike with high–speed jets,
a Waterpik, a Cuisinart
and a hypo–allergenic dog.
I want all the luxuries of the modern age,
and every item on every page
in the Lillian Vernon catalogue.

LUTHER: *"Oh baby, something's crossed my mind*
And I was thinking you'd look so fine
in a velvet dress
with heels and an ermine stole."

HANSEL: *"Oh, Luther darling, heaven knows*
I've never put on women's clothes
except for once
my mother's camisole."

So you think only a woman
can truly love a man.
Then you buy me the dress
I'll be more woman
than a man like you can stand.
I'll be your Venus on a chocolate clam shell
rising on a sea of marshmallow foam
and if you got some sugar for me,
Sugar Daddy, bring it home.

It's our tradition to control,
Like Erich Honecker and Helmut Kohl,
From the Ukraine to the Rhone.
Sweet home über alles,
Lord, I'm coming home
So come on, Sugar Daddy, bring me home.

(She whips out an American flag for the big finish.)

It wasn't a traditional wedding. For example, when Luther popped
the question, I was on my knees. I invited him home for dinner—

(Fanning herself, she opens the emergency door for air.
The concert barges in again.)

41

TOMMY
—me, the real me, the me I used to be—

(She closes the door quickly.)

HEDWIG
After dessert, Luther produces a ring, an application for American citizenship, and a wig.

> (HANSEL:) "He loves me, mother. He wants to marry me and get me the hell out of here."

I put the wig on my head. It's a hideous beige shag.

> (HANSEL:) "Mother, is this so crazy it just might work?"

Mother's face might have been a photograph it was so still. After what seemed like a lifetime . . . probably hers . . . she reaches out her hand to straighten the wig.

> (MOTHER:) "Get me my passport and my camera, Hansel. I know a certain party."

Yes, the party she'd be having after I left.

> (MOTHER:) It's a simple cut and paste job. We change the photo and you can use my name, Hedwig Schmidt."

(LUTHER:) "Not so simple, ladies. Baby, you know I love you. I'm always thinking of you. But I got to marry you here. In East Berlin. And that means a full physical examination."

(HANSEL:) "Why, they'll see right away that—

(LUTHER:) "Baby. To walk away, you gotta leave something behind. Am I right, Mrs. Schmidt?"

(MOTHER:) "I've always thought so, Luther. Hansel, to be free, one must give up a little part of oneself. And I know just the doctor to take it. *(points a camera at* HANSEL*)* Don't move!"

(camera flash)

THE ANGRY INCH

My sex–change operation got botched
My guardian angel fell asleep on the watch
Now all I got is a Barbie Doll–crotch
I got an angry inch

Six inches forward and five inches back
I got a
I got an angry inch
Six inches forward and five inches back
I got a
I got an angry inch

I'm from the land where you still hear the cries
I had to get out, had to sever all ties
I changed my name and assumed a disguise
I got an angry inch

Six inches forward and five inches back
I got a
I got an angry inch
Six inches forward and five inches back
I got a
I got an angry inch
Six inches forward and five inches back
The train is coming and I'm tied to the track
I try to get up but I can't get no slack
I got a
Angry Inch Angry Inch

My mother made my tits out of clay
My boyfriend told me that he'd take me away
They dragged me to the doctor one day
I've got an angry inch

Six inches forward and five inches back
I got a
I got an angry inch
Six inches forward and five inches back
I got a
I got an angry inch

Long story short
When I woke up from the operation
I was bleeding down there
I was bleeding from the gash between my legs
My first day as a woman
and already it's that time of the month
But two days later
the hole closed up.
The wound healed
and I was left with a one inch mound of flesh
where my penis used to be
where my vagina never was.
A one inch mound of flesh with a scar running down it
like a sideways grimace
on an eyeless face
Just a little bulge
It was an angry inch

Six inches forward and five inches back
The train is coming and I'm tied to the track
I try to get up but I can't get no slack
I got an
Angry Inch Angry Inch

Six inches forward and five inches back
stay under cover till the night turns to black
I got an inch and I'm set to attack
I got an Angry Inch Angry Inch

YITZHAK

November 9, 1988. A tiny registrar's office with a breathtaking view over the Wall. Herr Hansel Schmidt becomes Mrs. Hedwig Robinson.

(A projected little HANSEL *gains a wig and dress.)*

HEDWIG

Tomorrow I am leaving on a jet plane and by the time I get to Phoenix love will keep us together. *(singing from* I am Woman*)* 'Cause I'm just an embryo, with a long, long way to go, but I know too much to go back and pretend!

YITZHAK

November 9, 1989. Junction City, Kansas.

HEDWIG

I sit in my mobile home, and on bootleg cable, watch the Wall come down. Divorced, penniless, a woman. I cry, because I will laugh if I don't.

Suddenly, I miss Mother. I consider calling Berlin, but then remember with envy her recent escape to sunny Yugoslavia. Perhaps Luther would be home. No, he was never the one. Never the missing half.

I catch myself in a mirror and for the first time see clearly the horror hunkering on my head. The same carpet remnant that Luther presented to me a year ago to disguise my receding . . . receding . . . I'm receding. I tear the wig from my scalp and hurl it across the room at a pile of unopened anniversary presents.

(lights soften, mournful piano intro begins)

There it lies, feigning shock. My personal hair system. My personal hell. My hedwig.

WIG IN A BOX

On nights like this
when the world's a bit amiss
and the lights go down
across the trailer park
I get down
I feel had
I feel on the verge of going mad
and then it's time to punch the clock
I put on some make–up
and turn up the tape deck
and pull the wig down on my head
suddenly I'm Miss Midwest
Midnight Checkout Queen
until I head home
and put myself to bed

I look back on where I'm from
look at the woman I've become
and the strangest things
seem suddenly routine
I look up from my Vermouth on the rocks

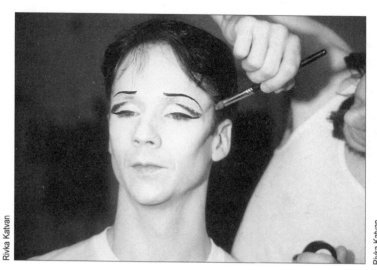

Rivka Katvan

Rivka Katvan

a gift–wrapped wig still in the box
of towering velveteen
I put on some make–up
and some LaVern Baker
and pull the wig down from the shelf
Suddenly I'm Miss Beehive 1963
Until I wake up
and turn back to myself

Some girls they have natural ease
they wear it any way they please
with their French flip curls
and perfumed magazines
Wear it up
Let it down

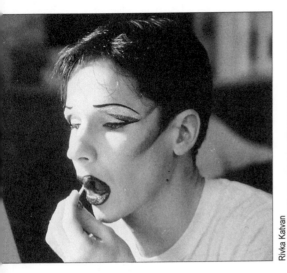

Rivka Katvan

This is the best wig that I've found
to be the best you've ever seen

I put on some make–up
and turn up the eight–track
I'm pulling the wig down from the shelf
Suddenly I'm Miss Farrah Fawcett
from TV
until I wake up
and I turn back to myself

Shag, bi-level, bob
Dorothy Hamill do,
Sausage curls, chicken wings
It's all because of you

With your blow dried, feather back,
Toni home wave, too
flip, fro, frizz, flop

It's all because of you
It's all because of you
It's all because of you

(The lyrics of the chorus are projected for all to sing.
YITZHAK *adds the extension to* HEDWIG's *wig. She changes*
into a fabulous new dress.)

I put on some make–up
and turn up the eight–track
I'm pulling the wig down from the shelf
Suddenly I'm this punk rock star

Rivka Katvan

of stage and screen

and I ain't never

I'm never turning back

(YITZHAK *helps* HEDWIG *on with a fur coat.*)

Thank you. I think we have our single! *(spits beer into audience)* That was a rock and roll gesture. Actually that was a heavy metal gesture. Want to see a punk rock gesture? *(fills mouth with beer; a threatening pause; then she spits it all over herself)* It's the direction of the aggression that defines it. How 'bout this band? On bass, Jacek; on drums, Schlatko; on guitar, Krzyzhtoff; and my trusted musical director, Skszp! So very talented. And so very lucky to be here. Right, boys?

BAND

Yes, Miss Hedwig.

Rivka Katvan

Rivka Katvan

HEDWIG

Very good, boys. Let's watch the tempo next time. *(She models the fur coat.)* You like the pelt? Some bitch stopped me on the way in, "What poor, unfortunate creature had to die for you to wear that?" "My Aunt Trudi," I replied.

> *(She turns to check her make-up—a large splotch of red paint is revealed on the back of the coat. An onstage pay phone starts to ring.)*

I told him to turn that off before the show. I should take this.
> (YITZHAK *carries the pay phone to her.)*

(to audience) Serbian cell phone. *(into phone)* Hello? *(to audience)* It's my agent, Phyllis Stein. *(an exciting private conversation; she hangs up)* Guess who's the new spokeswoman for the Tourist Board of Greater Serbia? *(singing to the tune of* Happy Christmas*)* "Come back to Greater Serbia. Come Christian, come Jew. We hope you can join us. We've cleansed it for you."

I'm feeling a little isolated up here. Have I introduced my husband, Yitzhak? We met during my Great Croatian Tour of the early mid–nineties. He was the most famous drag queen in Zagreb. Phyllis thought he would make a great opening act. Billed as "The Last Jewess in the Balkans," he lipsynched something from *Yentl* under the name Krystal Nacht. He was good. He was too good. His applause drowned out my introduction and I refused to go on. But on my way out, he begged me to take him with me. My face might have been my mother's, it was so still. I said to him, "Krystal, to walk

away, you gotta leave something behind. I'll marry you on the condition that a wig never touch your head again." He agreed and we've been inseparable ever since. And we'll continue to be. Right, Yitzhak? *(pointing into the house)* Look, Yitzhak, immigration! *(*YITZHAK *doesn't look.)* Barbra Streisand! *(nothing)* You're no fun, go back to your hole. (YITZHAK *goes.)* Ladies and gentlemen, I hope you are becoming fans of Hedwig. Because I find that *I* am certainly becoming a f—

YITZHAK

Cunt.

HEDWIG

(turns to the alley door)
Finally! Finally, Tommy's getting around to—

(She opens the door.)

TOMMY *(off)*

. . . me, me, me, me—

(She closes the door. Then opens it.)

TOMMY

. . . one day, this little trailer trash kid put on some of his mom's eyeliner, grabbed his beat–up J.C. Penney guitar and called himself Tommy Gnosis!

(She slams the door.)

HEDWIG

Tommy! Can you hear me? From this milkless tit, you sucked the very business we call show. *(to audience)* Okay. Okay. You want to know about Tommy Gnosis? I'll tell you about Tommy Gnosis. Get this dead thing off me.

> (YITZHAK *removes her fur coat and wig extension.* Hedwig *turns to the band.)*

LEUTE, WIR IMPROVISIEREN JETZT! BLEIBT DRAN!

After my divorce, I scraped by with babysitting gigs and odd jobs. Mostly the jobs we call blow. I had lost my job at the base PX and I had lost my gag reflex. You do the math. I sat for the baby of General Speck, commander of the nearby army fort. His other son was the Artist Formerly Known As My Buttboy.

> *(projection of drawing of* TOMMY)

Yes, Tommy Speck. Tommy was a seventeen–year–old, four–eyed, pock–marked, Dungeons and Dragons–obsessed Jesus freak with a fish on his truck and I found him incredibly hot. Perhaps it was his disdain for authority, his struggle with organized religion. One day, I walked in on him punishing the bishop.

He was in the bath with the door wide open, clearly waiting for me. I reached down, finished His Grace off, and dropped a flyer on the bathmat. "By the way, Tommy, I am performing a short set tonight at Dr. Espresso's Seattle–Style Coffee Enema Bar. Maybe I'll see you there." I had recently returned to my first love, music. I had tried singing once back in Berlin. They threw tomatoes. After the show I had a nice salad. But newly motivated, I bought a cheap electric piano. *(piano phrase from some cheesy hit)* That song was built in, it was so cheap. And I found a couple of Korean sargeants' wives who churned out a mean rhythm section. *(bad drums)* Somehow we became quite a draw singing the hits of the day under the name The Angry Inch.

(projection of Dr. Espresso's logo)

That night the audience was small but hostile.
(lounge version of Smells Like Teen Spirit *winds down)*

(to audience) Thank you. Both of you. That song was by Kurt Cobain. That kid's got a future, huh? And how 'bout Kwang-yi on guitar? Give it up! Kwang-yi! *(bad guitar solo)* Give it up, Kwang. Looks like we have a celebrity here tonight over by the Sweet & Low. Ladies and gentlemen, little Tommy Speck, the General's son! *(BAND claps half-heartedly.)* That's more than I got, honey. He's embarrassed. *(piano intro starts)* Well, I'm a little nervous myself. This is the first song I've ever written. And it's written for a guy to sing. We're talking to Phil Collins' people. But then aren't we all?

WICKED LITTLE TOWN

**You know, the sun is in your eyes
And hurricanes and rains
and black and cloudy skies.**

You're running up and down that hill.
You turn it on and off at will.
There's nothing here to thrill
or bring you down.
And if you've got no other choice
You know you can follow my voice
through the dark turns and noise
of this wicked little town.

Oh Lady, luck has led you here
and they're so twisted up
they'll twist you up. I fear

the pious, hateful and devout,
you're turning tricks til you're turned out,
the wind so cold it burns,
you're burning out and blowing round.
And if you've got no other choice
you know you can follow my voice
through the dark turns and noise
of this wicked little town.

The fates are vicious and they're cruel.
You learn too late you've used two wishes
like a fool

and then you're someone you are not,
and Junction City ain't the spot,

remember Mrs. Lot
and when she turned around.
And if you got no other choice
you know you can follow my voice
through the dark turns and noise
of this wicked little town.

(She blows a kiss to TOMMY *on the final chord. She dabs
her face with a towel and looks down at it. She holds it up.)*

The shroud of Hedwig, ladies and gentlemen.

The next day, I was putting the little Speck baby to bed when
Tommy appeared with a very expensive–looking electric guitar.

(TOMMY:) "Your show . . . that song . . . my dad . . . gave me this
guitar to apologize for being a pathetic little dictator. You want
to come up to my room?"

We went up to the attic and he sang me songs. "Classics," I was
informed. The bands were new to me: Boston, Kansas, America,
Europe, Asia. I put my hand on his strings. "Travel exhausts me."

(TOMMY:) "Where are you from, Hedwig?"

I told him my story. His face might have been a Yes album cover it
was so still.

(TOMMY:) "Have you accepted Jesus Christ, the Son of God, as your personal savior?"

I told him I was aware of Our Lord. Loved His work.

(TOMMY:) "You know, what He saved us from was His fucking father. I mean what kind of God creates Adam in His image, pulls Eve out of him to keep him company, and then tells them not to eat from the Tree of Knowledge? That was so micromanaging. So was Adam. But Eve. Eve just wanted to know shit. She took a bite of the apple and found out what was good and what was evil. And she gave it to Adam so he would know. Because they were in love. And that was good they now knew. Hedwig, will you give me the apple?"

The words spilling from those lips. And his eyes. His irises were clear cylinders of surprising depth. And emptiness. Only a few puddles of bluish pain sloshed around inside. Same blue as my eyes.

(Acoustic guitar and projections accompany the following.)

At the time, Tommy's performance options were limited to the occasional guitar mass. I initiated a six month curriculum of rock history, lyrics, grooming and vocal training—my patented oven technique. For his graduation, I gave him his name, Tommy Gnosis *(The word is projected.)*, the Greek word for knowledge. We collaborated. Songs exploded out of us. He started singing backup for me at Dr. Espresso's. Teenage girls started showing up. I added a few duets. Standing–room only. Then, the Sizzler called. In three months, we were outgrossing monster trucks in Wichita. With that kind of money coming in, I was able to give up all my jobs and devote myself entirely to our career. We were very happy.

One day, I am curled up in the trailer with my usual late-afternoon constitutional of grain alcohol and Brita. I like to be good to myself. Suddenly, Tommy is at the door in tears.

(HEDWIG:) "Honey, what is it?"

(TOMMY:) "My dad . . . and my mom . . . and my parents."
I hold him as I never had been held. But as usual he squirms, slides behind me and clutches my spine to his chest. I am suddenly very much aware that we haven't kissed in all the months we've been together. In fact, he has maintained a near-perfect ignorance of the front of me. Perhaps because of his preference for over–the–shoulder love.

Carol Rosegg

(projection of HEDWIG's *and* TOMMY's *figures in a "spooning" position)*

(HEDWIG:) "Honey, why don't you work on that new song while I finish shaving your eyebrows?"

(guitar)

(TOMMY *sings:)* "Look what you done . . . *(The chord is wrong.)* Shit."

Another song blows in from the trailer next door.

YITZHAK

(sings I Will Always Love You *à la Whitney Houston)*
. . . and IIIIIIIII . . .

HEDWIG

This song has been playing on a loop for three days.

YITZHAK

. . . . will always love you. I will always love you . . .

HEDWIG

Tommy looks up at me through new lenses, one blue and one pink.

(TOMMY:) "What do you think? Does love last forever?"

(HEDWIG:) "No, but this song does."

(TOMMY:) "Do not knock a multiplatinum single. I wish I could hit those notes."

(HEDWIG:) "Just move your lips and I'll sing them for you, honey. From a shadowy corner of the stage. Like Mick Jagger's back-up singer."

We laugh at the professional reference. I return to his brows.

YITZHAK

(singing)
But most of all I wish you love . . .

HEDWIG

(HEDWIG:) "Seriously, Tom, yes. I believe love is immortal."
(guitar chords)

(TOMMY *sings:*) "Look what you done . . . *(bad chord)* god-dammit! How is it immortal?"

(HEDWIG:) "Well, perhaps because love creates something that was not there before."

(TOMMY:) "What, like procreation?"

(HEDWIG:) "Yes, but not only."

(TOMMY:) "What, like recreation?"

He grabs my ass and he laughs. I don't.

(HEDWIG:) "Sometimes just creation. Don't move."

I paint a bold silver cross on his forehead.

(guitar chords)

(HEDWIG:) "Honey, have you thought of a B flat after that B?"

(chords)

(TOMMY *sings:*) "Look what you done—"

Rivka Katvan

Rivka Katvan

Carol Rosegg

Photos, center spread and last page Rivka Katvan

(The B flat works gloriously. TOMMY *looks up at her in awe.)*

YITZHAK

(modulating)
And IIIIII! . . .

*(*YITZHAK *continues to sing through the following.)*

HEDWIG

Tommy slowly rises and draws the curtains that are attached at the top and the bottom. He reachs out his hand. I take it. I notice how well his "Harlem Spice" nail color complements my own "Dusty Menses". He spins me into his arms and rubs his pelvis . . . into the small of my back.

*(*TOMMY *sings:)* "Look what you done. You made me whole. Before I met you, I was the song. But now I'm the video."

*(*HEDWIG *sings:)* "Look what I've done. I made you whole. You know that you were just a ham. Then came me, the Dole . . . pineapple rings."

He laughs and I am filled with an ancient clarity. He's the one.

*(*ORIGIN OF LOVE *chords. A projection appears of two complementary faces—one male, one female—familiar from* The Origin of Love *sequence.)*

No blood in my eyes, no blood on his face. He's the one. The one who was taken. The one who left. The twin born by fission. He'll die in fusion, our fusion, cold fusion, unlimited power, unlimited knowledge, the secrets he must hold, the memories that we shared but are now forgotton, the words to complete the sentence that I began, "I am . . . !" My eyes fill with muddy Maybelline tears.

> (TOMMY:) "Oh, Hedwig. Oh, God. When Eve was still inside Adam, they were in Paradise. When she was separated from him, that's when Paradise was lost. So when she enters him again, Paradise will be regained!"

> (HEDWIG:) "That's right, however you want it, honey, just kiss me while we do it."

I wrench my body around to face him and thrust his hand between my legs—

> (TOMMY:) "What is that?"

> *(pause)*

> (HEDWIG:) "That's what I have to work with."

> *(pause)*

> (TOMMY:) "My mom is probably wondering where I—"

> (HEDWIG:) "Sissy. Nancy, girly, lispyboy. What are you afraid of?"

(TOMMY:) "I love you."

(HEDWIG:) "Then love the front of me."

He runs out the back door.

(Guitar intro. HEDWIG *tries to sing but cannot. Silence. Her accompanist,* SKSZP, *begins to sing.)*

THE LONG GRIFT

Look what you've done,
you gigolo.
You know that I loved you, hon,
and I didn't want to know
that your cool,
seductive serenade
was a tool
of your trade,
you gigolo.

Of all the riches you've surveyed,
and all that you can lift,
I'm just another dollar that you made
in your long, long grift

(HEDWIG *removes her wig to reveal a shorter, crueler one beneath. She joins* YITZHAK *and sings backup with him.)*

Look what you've done,

you gigolo.

Another hustle has been run,

and now you ought to know

that this fool

can no longer be swayed

by the tools

of your trade,

you gigolo.

I'm just another john you've gypped,

another sucker stiffed,

a walk–on role in the script

to your long, long grift.

The love that had me in your grip

was just a long, long grift.

(HEDWIG *studies* YITZHAK *with new interest.*)

HEDWIG

It's nice over here. Out of the spotlight. You and me. Singing back-up in our oven. Couple of survivors. The German and the Jew. Think of the symmetry. Think of the power. Think of the publicity. The gods would be terrified.

(HEDWIG *goes to kiss* YITZHAK. *He spits in her face and walks away.*)

HEDWIG'S LAMENT

I was born on the other side
of a town ripped in two
And no matter how hard I've tried
I end up black and blue

I rose from off of the doctor's slab
I lost a piece of my heart
Now everyone gets to take a stab
They cut me up into parts

I gave a piece to my mother
I gave a piece to my man
I gave a piece to the rock star
He took the good stuff and ran

EXQUISITE CORPSE

Oh God
I'm all sewn up
A hardened razor–cut
Scar map across my body
And you can trace the lines
Through Misery's design
That map across my body

Rivka Katvan

A collage
All sewn up
A montage
All sewn up

Rivka Katvan

A random pattern with a needle and thread
The overlapping way diseases are spread
Through a tornado body
With a hand grenade head
And the legs are two lovers entwined

Inside I'm hollowed out
Outside's a paper shroud
And all the rest's illusion
That there's a will and soul
That we can wrest control
From chaos and confusion

A collage
All sewn up
A montage
All sewn up

The automatist's undoing
The whole world starts unscrewing
As time collapses and space warps
You see decay and ruin
I tell you "No, no, no, no

You make such an exquisite corpse"

I've got it all sewn up
A hardened razor cut
Scar map across my body
And you can trace the lines
Through Misery's design
That map across my body

A collage
All sewn up
A montage
All sewn up

(She tears open her dress and pulls two tomatoes from her bra. She smashes them on her body and crumples to the floor. The BAND *glories in her collapse. The music crescendoes, disintegrates and crossfades to stadium-sized cheers.* HEDWIG's *body lies motionless. The piano intro to* WICKED LITTLE TOWN *begins as the glowing word* GNOSIS *fills the upstage wall.)*

TOMMY (*off*)

Before I go, I'd like to sing a song that someone wrote for me a long time ago. I don't know where she is tonight. But if you're real quiet . . . maybe she can hear me.

*(*HEDWIG *rises into new light, a bold silver cross shining on her brow. She has become* TOMMY *in concert.)*

WICKED LITTLE TOWN (reprise)

Forgive me,
For I did not know.
'Cause I was just a boy
And you were so much more

Than any god could ever plan,
More than a woman or a man.

Rivka Katvan

73

And now I understand
How much I took from you:
That, when everything starts breaking down,
You take the pieces off the ground
And show this wicked town
something beautiful and new.

You think that Luck
Has left you there.
But maybe there's nothing
Up in the sky but air.

And there's no mystical design,
No cosmic lover preassigned.
There's nothing you can find
that cannot be found.
'Cause, with all the changes
you've been through,
It seems the stranger's always you,
Alone again in some new
Wicked little town.

So, when you've got no other choice
You know you can follow my voice
Through the dark turns and noise
Of this wicked little town.
Oh, it's a wicked little town.
Goodbye, wicked little town.

(The ballroom lighting is restored. Silence. HEDWIG/TOMMY nods to the band. A guitar intro begins. The projection of the two complementary faces from The Origin of Love appears. HEDWIG retrieves the wig extension and begins to sing.)

MIDNIGHT RADIO

Rain falls hard
Burns dry
A dream
Or a song
That hits you so hard
Filling you up
And suddenly gone

(She holds the wig out to YITZHAK. With a sigh, YITZHAK takes it and begins to put it on HEDWIG's head. HEDWIG stops him. YITZHAK hesitates, then places the wig on his own head.)

Breathe Feel Love
Give Free
Know in your soul
Like your blood knows the way
From your heart to your brain
Know that you're whole

*(HEDWIG begs YITZHAK's hand. He grants it and they dance.
She releases his hand, setting him free. YITZHAK is bewildered
at first. Then he slowly descends the stage and exits into the
house with the grace of new hope. HEDWIG waves goodbye.)*

*And you're shining
Like the brightest star
A transmission
On the midnight radio
And you're spinning
Like a 45
Ballerina
Dancing to your rock and roll*

*Here's to Patti
    and Tina
    and Yoko
       Aretha
    and Nona
    and Nico
    and me*

*And all the strange rock and rollers
You know you're doing all right
So hold on to each other
You gotta hold on tonight
And you're shining
Like the brightest stars*

A transmission
On the midnight radio

And you're spinning
Your new 45s
All the misfits and the losers
Yeah, you know you're rock and rollers
Spinning to your rock and roll

Lift up your hands

(The upstage door opens under its own power. Bright light and enormous cheers flood the stage. HEDWIG blows a kiss to the audience and walks through the door into the light. The projected male and female faces merge into a single one.)

ARISTOPHANES' SPEECH
from PLATO'S *SYMPOSIUM*

In the first place, let me treat of the nature of man and what has happened to it; for the original human nature was not like the present, but different. The sexes were not two as they are now, but originally three in number; there was man, woman and the union of the two, having a name corresponding to this double nature, which had once a real existence, but is now lost, and the word "Androgynous" is only preserved as a term of reproach. In the second place, the primeval man was round, his back and sides forming a circle; and he had four hands and four feet, one head with two faces, looking opposite ways, set on a round neck and precisely alike; also four ears, two privy members, and the remainder to correspond. He could walk upright as men now do, backwards or forwards as he pleased, and he could also roll over and over at a great pace, turning on his four hands and four feet, eight in all, like tumblers going over and over with their legs in the air; this was when he wanted to run fast. Now the sexes were three; and such as I have described them; because the sun, moon and earth are three and the man was originally the child of the sun, the woman of the earth, and the man-woman of the moon, which is made up of sun and earth, and they were all round and moved round and round like their parents. Terrible was their might and strength, and the thoughts of their hearts were great, and they made an attack upon the gods; of them is told the tale of Otys and Ephialtes who, as Homer says, dared to scale heaven, and would have laid hands upon the gods. Doubt reigned in the celestial councils. Should they kill them and annihilate the race with thunderbolts, as they had done the giants, then there would be an end of the sacrifices and worship which men offered to them; but, on the other hand, the gods could not suffer their insolence to be unrestrained. At last, after a good deal of reflection, Zeus discovered a way. He said: "Methinks I have a plan which will humble their pride and improve their manners; men shall continue to exist, but I will cut them in two and then they will be diminished in strength and increased in numbers; this will have the advantage of making them more profitable to us. They shall walk upright on two legs, and if they continue insolent and will not be quiet, I will split them again, and they shall hop about on a single leg." He spoke and cut men in two, like a sorb-apple which is halved for pickling, or as you might divide an egg with a hair; and as he cut them one after another, he bade Apollo give the face and the half of the neck a turn in order that the man might contemplate the section of himself: he would thus learn a lesson of humility. Apollo was also bidden to heal their wounds and compose their forms. So he gave a turn to the face and pulled the skin from the sides all over that which in our language is called the belly, like the purses which draw in, and he made one mouth at the center, which he fastened in a knot (the same which is called the navel); he also molded the breast and took out most of the wrinkles, much as a shoemaker might smooth leather upon a last; he left a few, however, in the region of the belly and navel, as a memorial of the primeval state. After the division the two parts of man, each desiring his other half, came together, and throwing their arms about one another, entwined in mutual embraces, longing to grow into one, they were on the point of dying from hunger and self-neglect, because they did not like to do anything apart; and when one of the halves died and the other survived, the survivor sought another mate, man or woman as we call them,—being the sections of entire men or women,—and clung to that. They were being destroyed, when Zeus in pity of them invented a new plan: he turned the parts of generation round to the front, for this had not been always their position, and they sowed the seed no longer as hitherto like grasshoppers in the ground, but in one another; and after the transposition the male generated in the female in order that by the mutual embraces of man and woman they might breed, and the race might continue; or if man came to man they might be satisfied, and rest, and go their ways to the business of life: so ancient is the desire of one another which is implanted in us, reuniting our original nature, making one of two, and healing the state of man. Each of us when separated, having one side only, like a flat fish, is but the indenture of a man, and he is always looking for his other half. Men who are a section of that double nature which was once called Androgynous are lovers of women; adulterers are generally of this breed, and also adulterous women who lust after men: the women who are a section of the woman do not care for men, but have female attachments; the female companions are of this sort. But they who are a section of the male follow the male, and while they are young, being slices of the original man, they hang about men and embrace them, and they are themselves the best of boys and youths, because they have the most manly nature. Some indeed assert that they are shameless, but this is not true: for they do not act thus from any want of shame, but because they are valiant and manly, and have a manly countenance, and they embrace that which is like them. And these when they grow up become our statesmen, and these only, which is a great proof of the truth of what I am saying. When they reach manhood they are lovers of youth, and are not naturally inclined to marry or beget children,—if at all, they do so only in obedience to the law; but they are satisfied if they may be allowed to live with one another unwedded; and such a nature is prone to love and ready to return love, always embracing that which is akin to him. And when one of them meets with his other half, the actual half of himself, whether he be a lover of youth or a lover of another sort, the pair are lost in amazement of love and friendship and intimacy, and one will not be out of the other's sight, as I may say, even for a moment: these are the people who pass their whole lives together; yet they could not explain what they desire of one another. For the intense yearning which each of them has towards the other does not appear to be the desire of lover's intercourse, but of something else which the soul of either evidently desires and cannot tell, and of which she has only a dark and doubtful presentiment. Suppose Hephaestus, with his instruments, to come to the pair who are lying side by side and to say to them, "What do you people want of one another?" they would be unable to explain. And suppose further, that when he saw their perplexity he said: "Do you desire to be wholly one; always day and night to be in one another's company?

For if this is what you desire, I am ready to melt you into one and let you grow together, so that being two you shall become one, and while you live a common life as if you were a single man, and after your death in the world below still be one departed soul instead of two—I ask whether this is what you lovingly desire,—and whether you are satisfied to attain this?"—there is not a man of them who when he heard the proposal would deny or would not acknowledge that this meeting and melting into one another, this becoming one instead of two, was the very expression of his ancient need. And the reason is that human nature was originally one and we were a whole, and the desire and pursuit of the whole is called love. There was a time, I say, when we were one, but now because of the wickedness of mankind God has dispersed us, as the Arcadians were dispersed into villages by the Lacedaemonians. And if we are not obedient to the gods, there is a danger that we shall be split up again and go about in bas relief, like the profile figures having only half a nose which are sculptured on monuments, and that we shall be like tallies. Wherefore let us exhort all men to piety, that we may avoid evil, and obtain the good, of which love is to us the lord and minister; and let no one oppose him—he is the enemy of the gods who opposes him. For if we are friends of the God and at peace with him we shall find our own true loves. I believe that if our loves were perfectly accomplished, and each one returning to his primeval nature had his original true love, then our race would be happy.

Translated by Benjamin Jowett

CAST AND CREW

JOHN CAMERON MITCHELL *(Playwright, Hedwig, Tommy Gnosis)* appeared on Broadway in *The Secret Garden* (Drama Desk nomination), *Six Degrees of Separation*, and *Big River*. Off-Broadway credits include *The Destiny of Me* (Obie Award, Drama Desk nomination), *Hello Again* (Drama Desk nomination), and *Missing Persons*. John also adapted and directed Tennessee Williams' *Kingdom of Earth* for the Drama Dept. Theatre Co., of which he is a founding member. For writing and performing in *Hedwig*, John received an Obie Award, the Outer Critics Circle Award for Outstanding off-Broadway Musical, and Drama Desk nominations for Outstanding Actor in a Musical and for Outstanding New Musical. John is writing, directing and starring in the film adaptation of *Hedwig* (Killer Films and New Line Cinema).

STEPHEN TRASK *(Composer/Lyricist)* Stephen was one of the original members of the notorious Squeeze Box house band. During his time there as Music Director he performed with Debbie Harry, Lene Lovitch, Hole, Green Day, Joey Ramone, as well as many of New York's most popular drag queens. For five years Stephen performed with his band Cheater, who originated the role of *The Angry Inch* off-Broadway and performed on the original

cast recording. From 1993-1998, Stephen danced with and accompanied The Corner Store Dance Company. He has scored numerous dance pieces and movies. For *Hedwig*, Stephen received an Obie Award, the Outer Critics Circle Award for Outstanding off-Broadway Musical, a 1998 *New York* Magazine Award, Drama Desk nominations for Outstanding Music, Outstanding Lyrics, and Outstanding New Musical, Grammy nomination for Best Cast Album and two GLAMA Awards: Best Cast Album and Best Score for Film or Stage. He is currently producing an album for the rock band Nancy Boy as well as working on the film adaptation of *Hedwig*.

MIRIAM SHOR *(Yitzhak)* Miriam just finished shooting the feature film, *Bedazzled*, co-starring opposite Brendan Frazier. Her other film credits include the independent features *Entropy*, *Flushed* and *Snowy Days*. Upcoming, Miriam will be recreating the role of Yitzhak in the film version of *Hedwig*. Miriam can be seen as Cheryl in the ABC series *Then Came You*. She has also starred in numerous regional and national tour productions. Miriam played Yitzhak in New York and Los Angeles and can be heard on the Grammy nominated CD recording.

CHEATER *(The Angry Inch)* Before there was *The Angry Inch* there was Cheater, performing the songs of Stephen Trask (vocals/piano/guitar) and guitar icon Chris Weilding, propelled by the massive drums of Dave McKinley, and the panache of Scott Bilbrey (bass).

PETER ASKIN *(Director)* Stage: *Hedwig and the Angry Inch* (New York City, Boston, Los Angeles), *The Gimmick* (Sundance &

McCarter Theatre), *Political Animal, Beauty's Daughter* (Obie Award), *Spic-O-Rama* (NYC and Goodman Theatre, Drama Desk Award), *Mambo Mouth* (Obie Award, Outer Critics Circle Award). Other New York credits: *How It Hangs, Linda Her, Beauty Marks, Ourselves Alone, Reno, Down an Alley Filled with Cats.* Television: *House of Buggin'* (Supervising Producer) *Spic-O-Rama* (director, CableACE Award), WNET's *Bet One I Make It* (Producer/Director). Film: *Smithereens, Company Man. (Co-writer, Director), Old Scores* (pre-production).

JAMES YOUMANS *(Set Design)* designed *Hedwig* at the Westbeth Theatre. Other credits include *The Shaughraun* at Seattle Repertory Theatre and the Huntington Theatre, *The Country Club* at Long Wharf Theatre, *My Good Name* at the Bay Street Theatre Festival, *Finian's Rainbow* at the Goodspeed Opera House, *After Play* at MTC, Theatre Four, and Pasadena Playhouse; *Paper Moon* at the Goodspeed and Ford's Theatre; Randy Newman's *Faust* at La Jolla Playhouse; *Raised in Captivity* at the Vineyard Theatre and South Coast Rep (for which he won a Dramalogue Award); *The Swan and The Petrified Prince* (the latter for which he received a Drama Desk nomination) both at the New York Shakespeare Festival; *Swinging on a Star* on Broadway; *Jeffrey* in New York, L.A. and San Francisco; *Sight Unseen* both at the Orpheum and at Long Wharf Theatre. Other regional: Mark Taper Forum, Dallas Theatre Center, Arena Stage, Portland Stage, Virginia Stage.

FABIO TOBLINI *(Costume Design)* was born and raised in Verona, Italy. He studied fashion design in Milan and moved to New York City in 1991. He designed the original production of

Hedwig and the Angry Inch at Westbeth. Designs for opera include *Dido and Aeneas and La Cenerentola* at Caramoor Center for the Arts; *Deidamia, Tamerlano and Atalanta* at Manhattan School of Music and *Arlecchino* at Samar Staat Theatre, Russia. Among designs for theatre are *Red Noses* at Juilliard and productions of 1940's *Radio Hour* and *On Golden Pond* in stock. Fabio also designs costumes for several modern dance companies in New York City.

KEVIN ADAMS *(Lighting Design)* NYC: *Stupid Kids* (WPA); *Manhattan Music* (MTC); *Henry VI* (NYSF, Drama Desk nomination); *The Batting Cage* (Vineyard); scenery and lighting for Theatre Couture's *Tell-Tale* (Cherry Lane, P.S. 122); *Bad Sex with Bud Kemp* (also scenery, Second Stage); *Hot Mouth* (CSC, MTC); Sandra Bernhard's *Giving 'Til It Hurts* (Madison Square Garden Theatre); *The Nest* directed by Moisés Kaufman. Regional: *In Walks Ed* (Long Wharf, Cincinnati Playhouse), *An Almost Holy Picture* with David Morse (La Jolla, McCarter), Berkeley Rep, Trinity Rep, Old Globe, Spoleto Festival. Performance artists: Rachel Rosenthal, John Fleck, Han Ong. Film: *Without You I'm Nothing* (Art Director), Janet Jackson's music video *If* (Lighting Design). Mr. Adams is an internationally exhibited fine artist with work included in the permanent collections of the L.A. County Museum of Art. Mr. Adams is a graduate of Cal Arts.

WERNER F *(Sound Design)* Werner can be found touring with his band Vaporhead in support of their debut CD on Paradigm Records or writing music for television commercials and films or completing the score for the upcoming off-Broadway show *The Reborn Again Cowgirl* or . . . sleeping.

JERRY MITCHELL *(Musical Staging)* Jerry came up with a simple idea. Take the hottest Broadway dancers and give them a chance to live out a fantasy. That was the birth of *Broadway Bares,* New York's hotly anticipated yearly extravaganza featuring Broadway's most beautiful and talented dancers in an evening of song, dance, comedy and burlesque. Now in its eighth edition, *Broadway Bares* has continued to perform to sold-out houses and to raise money for Broadway Cares. Among his many choreography credits are *The Rosie O'Donnell Show* and the *VH-1 Music and Fashion Awards,* the film *In and Out, Follies* at the Paper Mill Playhouse and *Captains Courageous* at Manhattan Theatre Club.

MIKE POTTER *(Wig and Make-Up Design)* Currently residing in New York City, Mike Potter was born in rural Delaware. Raised in the conservative environment of the east coast, he sought creative refuge by destroying his grandmother's wigs from age six. In 1993, he received a Bachelor of Science in agricultural/resource economics from the University of Delaware. It was then he set out to London to work and travel. Michael also paints, writes, is the lead singer of his band. "Un-Tammy Set," and busies himself with making the meek and mild gorgeous.

JOE WITT *(Production Stage Manager)* Credits include: *Monster* by Obie-winner Dael Orlandersmith at New York Theatre Workshop; *Stonewall Jackson's House* at the American Place Theatre (a special consideration for the Pulitzer in Drama); *The Color of Love* at the Dorset Theatre Festival; *Angels in America* at the Vermont Stage Company; Ms. Orlandersmith's latest work, *The Gimmick,* which premiered at Sundance; at the McCarter Theatre; and was a Guest Artist at the University of Vermont,

where he taught Stage Management and Playwriting. NY: *Blown
Sideways Though Life* (Cherry Lane), *Lypsinka! A Day in the Life*
(Perry Street/Cherry Lane), *Owners & Traps* (New York Theatre
Workshop), *Slow Drag* (American Place). Regional: Adirondack
Theatre Festival, Snowmass Repertory Theatre Company, and six
seasons at Dorset Theatre Festival. Joe received his M.F.A. from
Columbia University and is a member of the Irish Repertory
Theatre.